# Folk Art Sampler Quilt

Pattern Designs by Evelyn Rose

Text by Rose Klix

FOLK ART SAMPLER QUILT

Published July 2018

Mountain Creek Press

All rights reserved

Copyright © 2018, Rose Klix, 3rd Edition

This book may not be reproduced in whole or part, in any manner whatsoever without written permission, with the exception of brief quotations within book reviews or articles.

Cover Photograph: The Folk Art Sampler Quilt by Evelyn Rose was one of the quilts featured in The Quilt Art '91 Engagement Calendar, published by The American Quilter's Society in 1991.

ISBN 13: 978-0-692-16836-3

ISBN 10: 0692168362

Library of Congress Control Number: 2018945925

# Table of Contents

| | |
|---|---:|
| Pattern List | 1 |
| Foreword – About Evelyn Rose | 3 |
| About Folk Art | 4 |
| The Folk Art Sampler Quilt | 5 |
| Quilt Size | 5 |
| Fabric Choices | 5 |
| Prewash Fabric | 6 |
| Cutting Background Squares, Triangles and Border Strips | 6 |
| About Templates | 41 |
| Placement of Appliqué | 41 |
| Marking and Cutting the Pattern Pieces | 41 |
| Basting | 42 |
| Appliqué Stitching | 42 |
| Setting | 43 |
| Preparing to Quilt | 44 |
| Feather Pattern | 46 |
| Finishing | 48 |
| Acknowledgments | 50 |
| About the Author | 51 |

# Pattern List

1. Floral Hex — 7
2. Sweetheart Bouquet — 9
3. Tulip Trio — 12
4. Ring of Hearts — 15
5. May Flowers — 17
6. Vase of Blooms — 19
7. Love Bird — 22
8. Butterfly — 25
9. Distelfink — 28
10. Thistledown — 31
11. Autumn Mums — 33
12. Holiday Tulips — 35
13. Border Templates — 37
14. Feather Pattern — 46

# Foreword – About Evelyn Rose

For over twenty years my mother, Evelyn Rose, owned and operated Pioneer Quilt Shop in Rapid City, South Dakota. Her shop was the only one in the state for several years. This was during a time of the quilt revivals in the mid-1970s.

In 1985 we published our first beginner book using her gentle technique to encourage students to progress from small to larger projects. We later expanded the first version and wrote two more special books for her students. They became out of print after she retired. Now I am so happy to share a reprint of these pattern and instruction books, especially this one for her special folk art quilt.

Mom started her cottage industry with a few students around a table in her home basement. The shop grew into a much larger location on Mount Rushmore Road. She attracted quilt enthusiasts from nearby states, tourists and visitors to the Black Hills. She said with a smile and twinkle in her eye, "My business supports my quilting habit."

The shop supplied 100% cotton fabric in rainbows of colors as well as every quilt tool available from her suppliers. She attended quilting workshops to learn more techniques and traveled to quilt markets and shows. The Fairfield Processing Corporation in Danfield, Connecticut photographed her Folk Art Sampler quilt for their full page batting advertisement on the back of quilt magazines. Mom was thrilled her Folk Art Sampler quilt was also featured on the February page of the American Quilters' Guild annual calendar for 1991.

Folk Art reminds me of Mother. Whether she was working on Cub Scout or Girl Scout art projects, doing her own version of tole painting, or designing other quilt patterns, she often combined folk art with her own creativity. She was truly an artist, who chose a fabric medium for her canvas. Mom called the shop's baskets of fat quarters her "palette of fabric colors and patterns." This book shows her choice of timeless folk art patterns which are beautiful in their simplicity and intricate symbolism.

I miss Mom every day. In 2009 her rest home nurse told me she died in her sleep shortly after they discussed a quilt project.

I encourage the reader to emulate Mom's style, use your imagination, and continue the legacy for your own unique love of quilting.

Peaceful Piecing,
Rose Klix

# About Folk Art

Basic folk art is woven into the fibers of our very existence. Its roots began in a simple way of life. Folk art themes are universal, although styles vary within each individual culture. Folk artists developed an appreciation for their surroundings and expressed their values of life through symbols.

Popular themes include flowers, animals, hearts, human figures in native and peasant costumes, birds and mythological figures. Bright colors, crude figure shapes, and simplicity in design all balanced to form the basic elements. Geometric shapes typically were used. The main design was centered without any background pattern provided. Instead borders surrounded and embellished the central design.

Folk art colors differed in various cultures. The Pennsylvania Dutch used subdued colors. South American and Scandinavian folk artists used less subtle combinations. Deeper reds and blues flavored Hungarian and Czechoslovakian colors. However, Hungarians freely used greens, yellows, and golds.

## Symbolic Meanings Include the Following Examples:

Bird looking at its tail = fruitfulness

Pineapple and acorn = symbols of colonial hospitality

Double eagle with centered heart = symbol of the Holy Roman Empire

Bird pecking at its breast = feeding of young

Three tulips or three stamens of lilies = Holy Trinity

Star = prosperity and fertility

Turtledove = love and human spirit

Peacock = resurrection of the dead

Unicorn = guardian of maidenhood

Blue-eyed animal or bird = Eye of God

Griffin (winged horse, half lion and half eagle) = strength and speed

The Pennsylvania Dutch chose religious motifs and symbols because they were extremely important to them. Hex designs were geometrical and star shaped. They were believed to ward off evil spirits and invoke blessings.

Several types of flowers were used. Tulips were prominent designs. Simple basic outlines of this graceful flower were widely copied and adapted. The lily, rose, daisy, violet, forget-me-not, anemone, fuchsia, carnation and clover were other popular designs.

Fruit forms include the apple, pear, grape, pineapple and pomegranate (love apple). Flowers and fruits were used as central designs and in border themes.

Bird designs include eagles, peacocks, pelicans, doves, swans, roosters, hens, parrots, herons, and the scarlet tanager. The mythical distilfink was popular. This resembled a two-headed robin looking backward.

Animals weren't forgotten and included rabbits, deer, lions, horses, lambs, dogs, unicorns and griffins.

Hearts were used liberally as central themes, for borders, or incorporated into designs.

# The Folk Art Sampler Quilt

This book showcases Evelyn Rose's choice of patterns for her Folk Art Sampler quilt. She shared her beautiful creation with local quilt enthusiasts who wished to practice appliqué or who simply enjoyed folk art. A 'Block of the Month' club was developed. As the name suggests each quilt maker was committed to completing one block per month. Mother helped them mark the pattern onto the background block and assisted some of the quilters with color choices. Template pieces and instructions were available with the pattern. Then we wrote a book of this pattern for a wider audience.

# Quilt Size

The finished quilt is approximately 82 inches wide by 106 inches long.

# Fabric Choices

Mom always suggested 100% cotton white muslin for the background blocks, filler blocks and border backgrounds. White backgrounds are recommended because it intrudes the least on the bright colors. However, other light-colored backgrounds possibly may be substituted.

Plan ahead for the backing fabric. Read the Finishing Section on page 34 for two binding choices which may impact the size of the backing fabric. Appliqué patterns use a variety of small scrap pieces in bright colors. Many of her students chose their colors from the fat quarters in the shop or from their own fabric scraps. Three or four greens are recommended for leaves, stems and vines on the blocks and borders. When sorting out colors to be used, choose the most colorful and brightest. However, fill in with colors which show a dramatic contrast. Solid colors may be used, but prints make the patterns more interesting and may add texture. Avoid light colors because the white background doesn't allow enough contrast.

# Prewash Fabric

It is <u>imperative</u> to prewash <u>all</u> the fabrics. 100% cotton tends to shrink but it is usually the best for appliqué stitching and quilting. Prewashing is especially true of any dark colors. The white background shows color 'bleeding' quite effectively. Prewashing avoids this problem.

# Cutting Background Squares, Triangles, and Border Strips

Cut eighteen 18-inch square blocks from the white muslin. Also cut ten 18 ¼ inch triangles. The long side (base) of the triangle should be cut on the straight grain to avoid fabric stretching when the triangles are set into the quilt. Cut four 12 ¼ inch triangles for the corners of the quilt. All the background measurements already include the ¼ inch seam allowance.

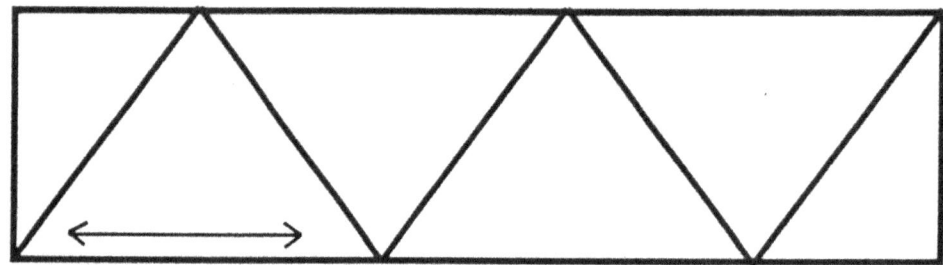

Cut the fabric for borders after all the blocks are set. Measure your quilt to ensure they fit. They should be approximately eight inches wide and 82 inches long for the top and bottom borders and approximately 106 inches long for the sides.

Note: You can cut four 18-inch blocks from one yard of 44 inch fabric. If the blocks are cut on the selvage side of the fabric, then the eight inch strips on the folded side may be used for borders.

# 1. Floral Hex (FH-)

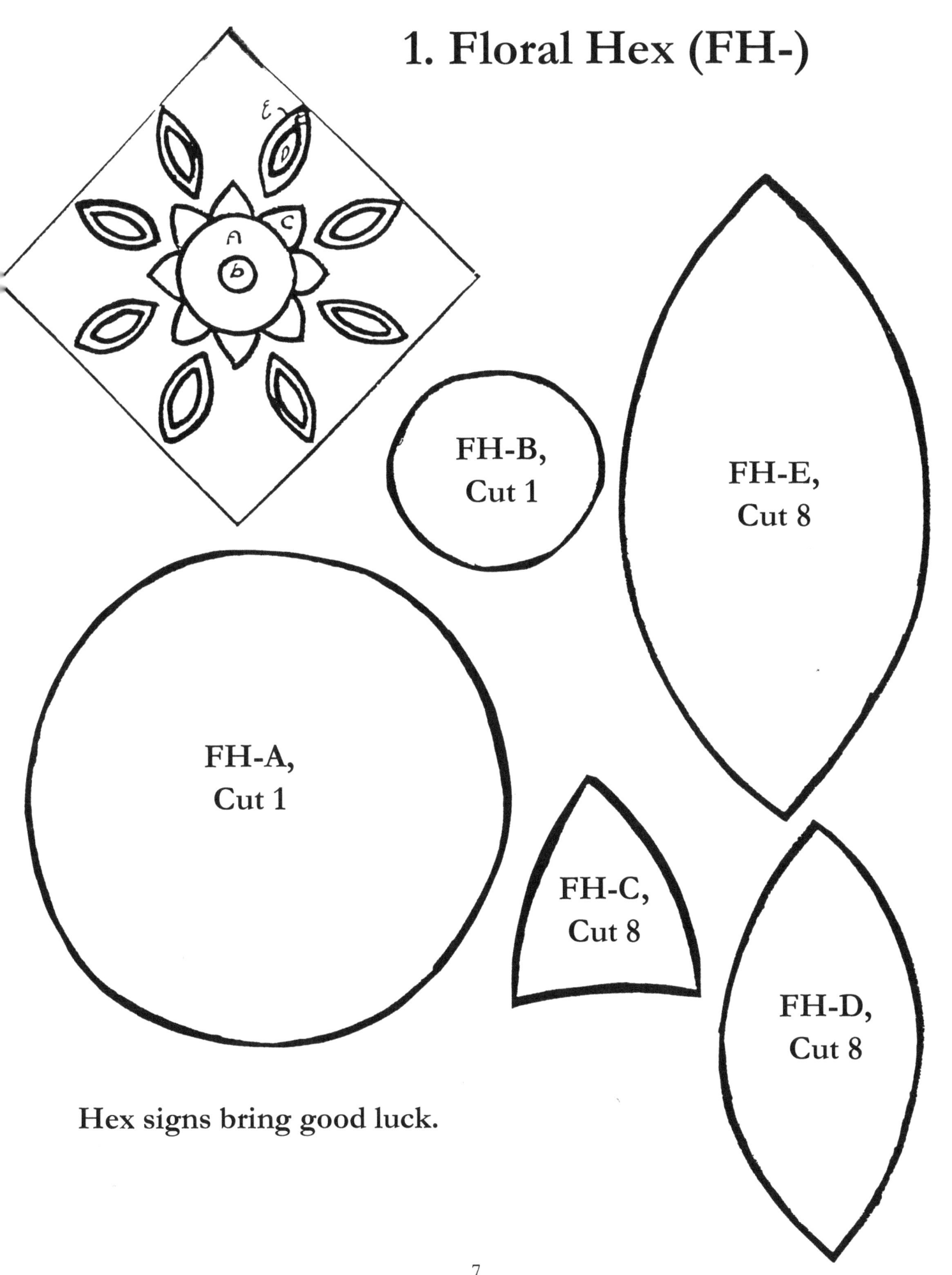

FH-B, Cut 1

FH-E, Cut 8

FH-A, Cut 1

FH-C, Cut 8

FH-D, Cut 8

Hex signs bring good luck.

# Floral Hex

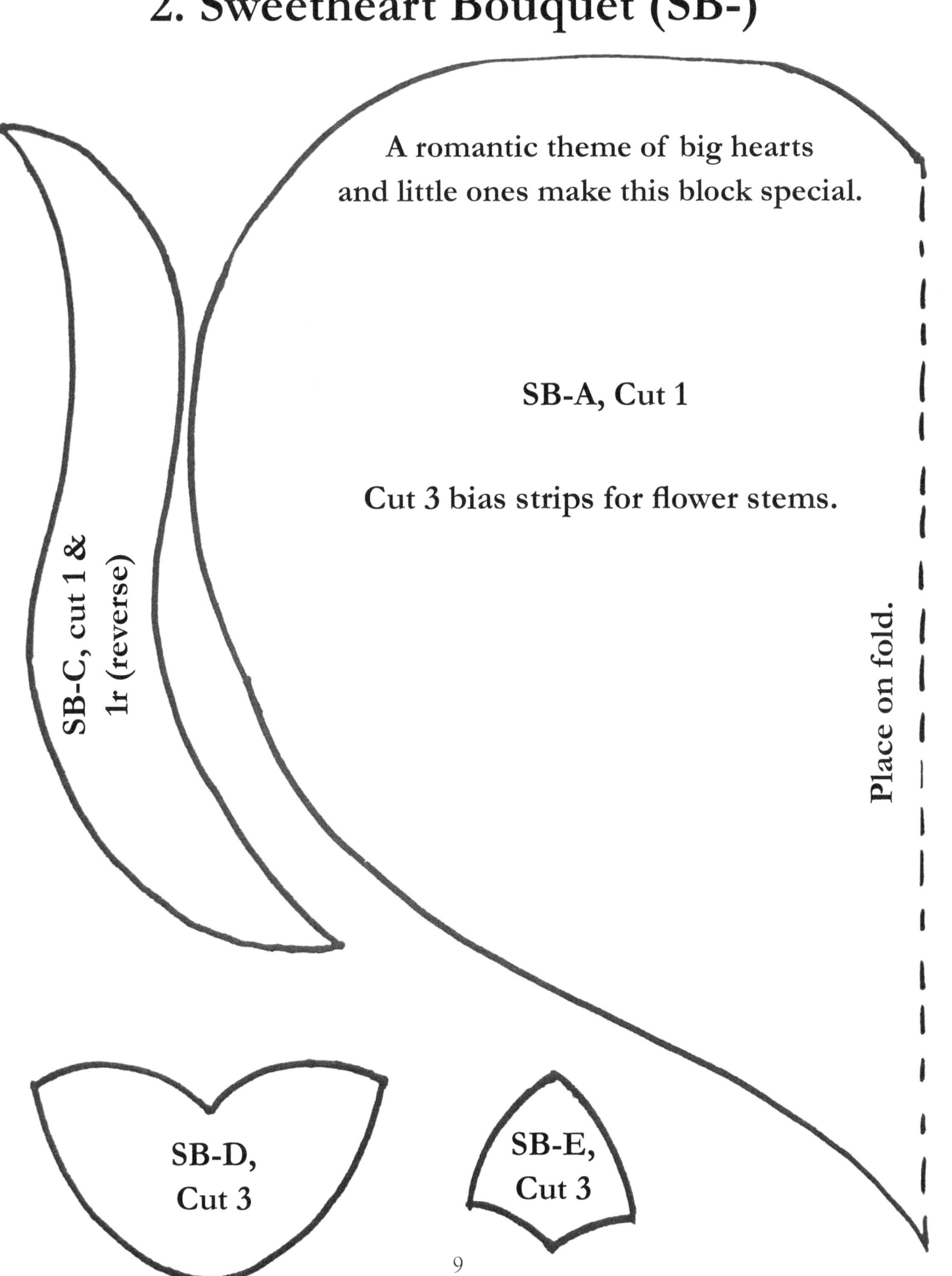

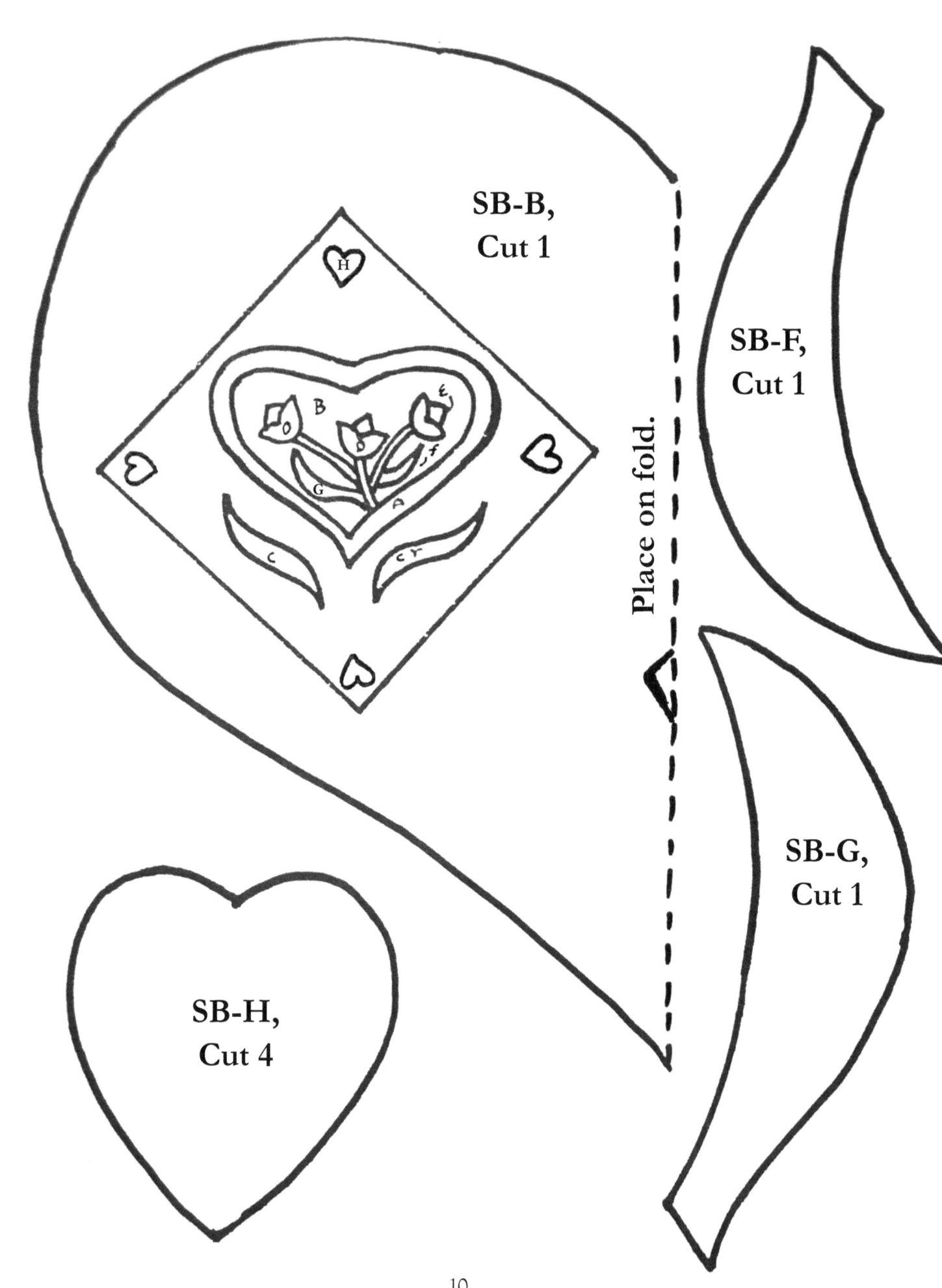

# Sweetheart Bouquet

# 3. Tulip Trio (TT-)

This tulip trio has its own plot of ground.

(TT-H) Make it brown or green.

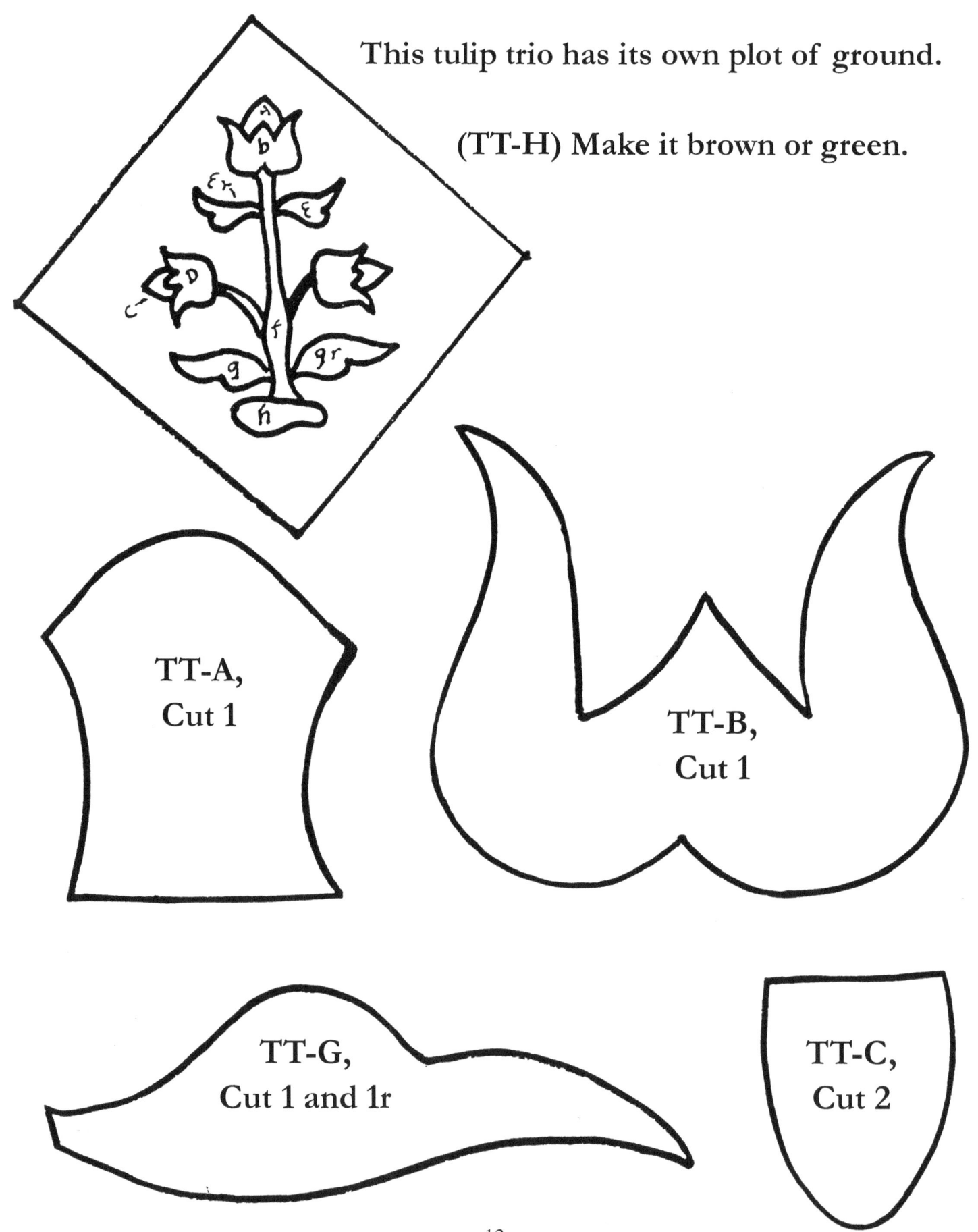

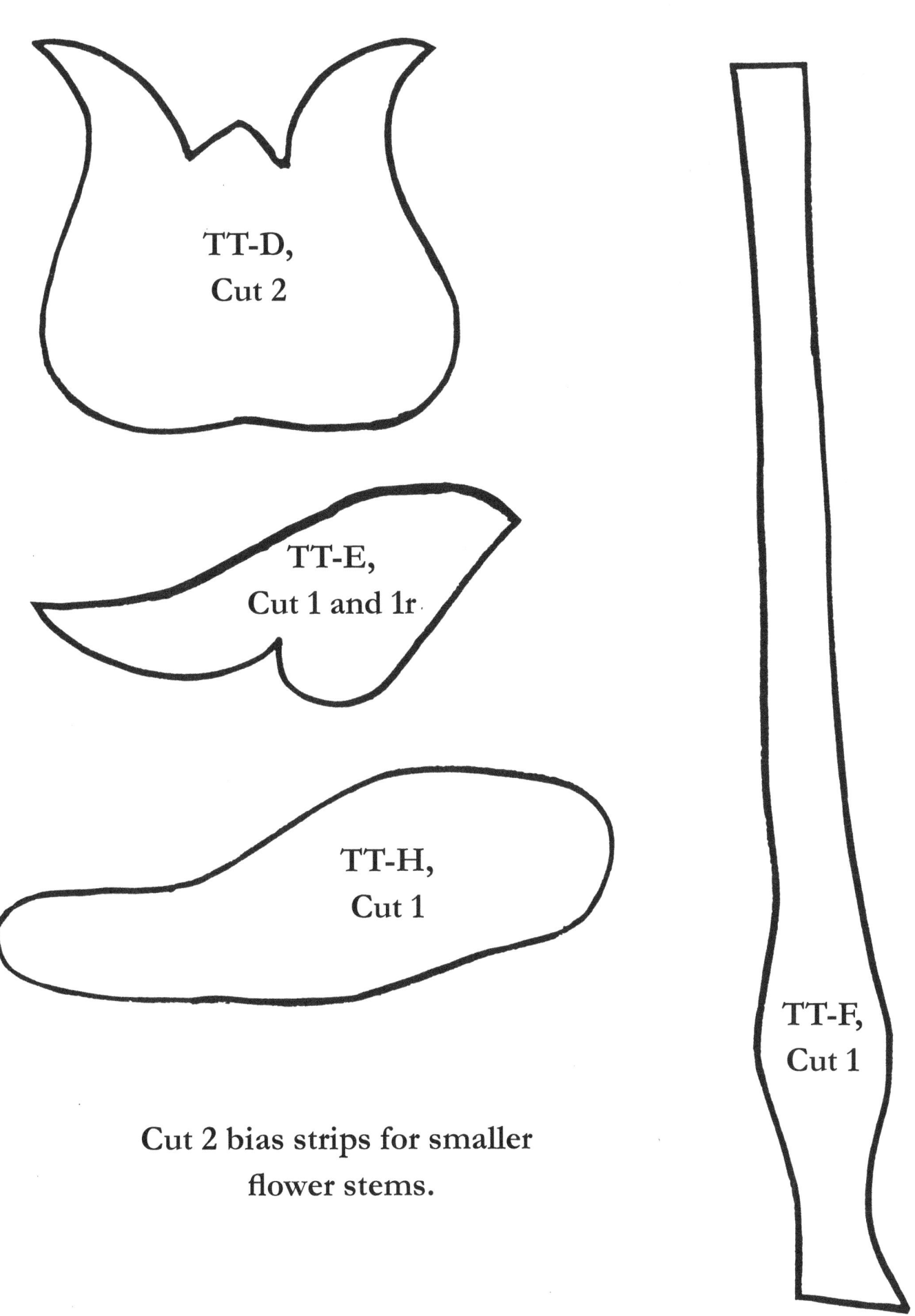

# Tulip Trio

# 4. Ring of Hearts (RH-)

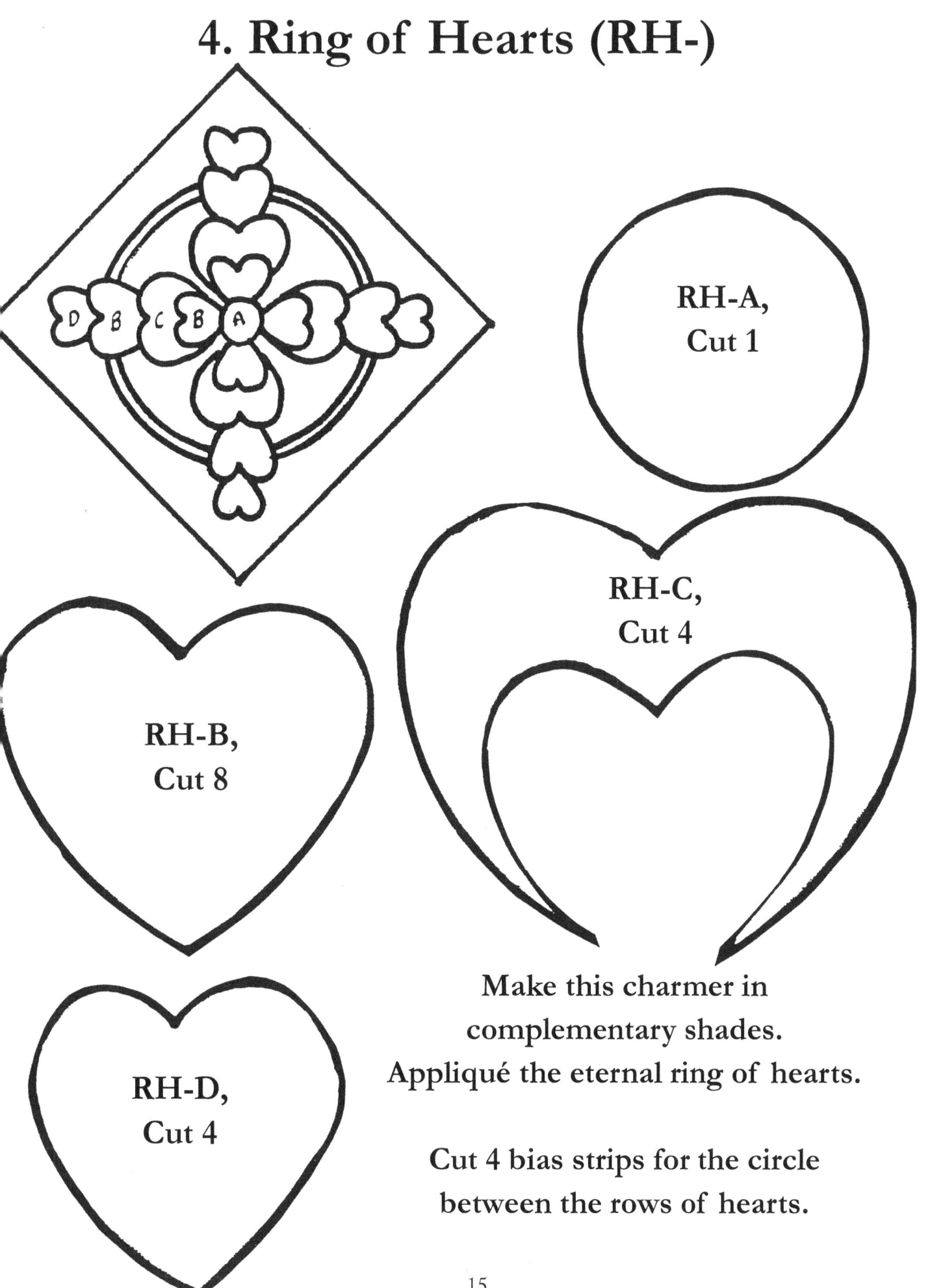

RH-A, Cut 1

RH-C, Cut 4

RH-B, Cut 8

RH-D, Cut 4

Make this charmer in complementary shades. Appliqué the eternal ring of hearts.

Cut 4 bias strips for the circle between the rows of hearts.

# Ring of Hearts

# 5. May Flowers (MF-)

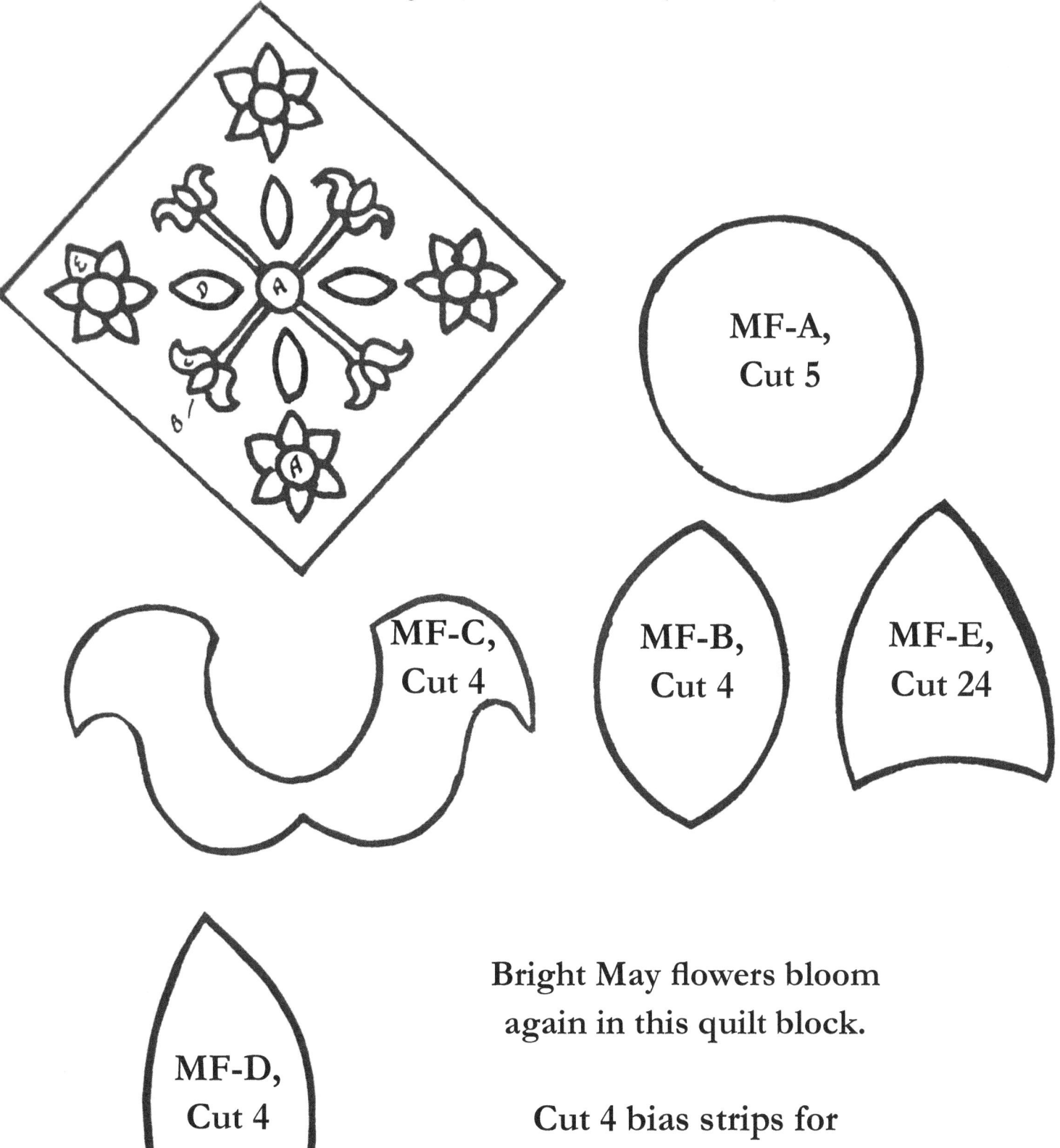

MF-A, Cut 5

MF-C, Cut 4

MF-B, Cut 4

MF-E, Cut 24

MF-D, Cut 4

Bright May flowers bloom again in this quilt block.

Cut 4 bias strips for flower stems.

# May Flowers

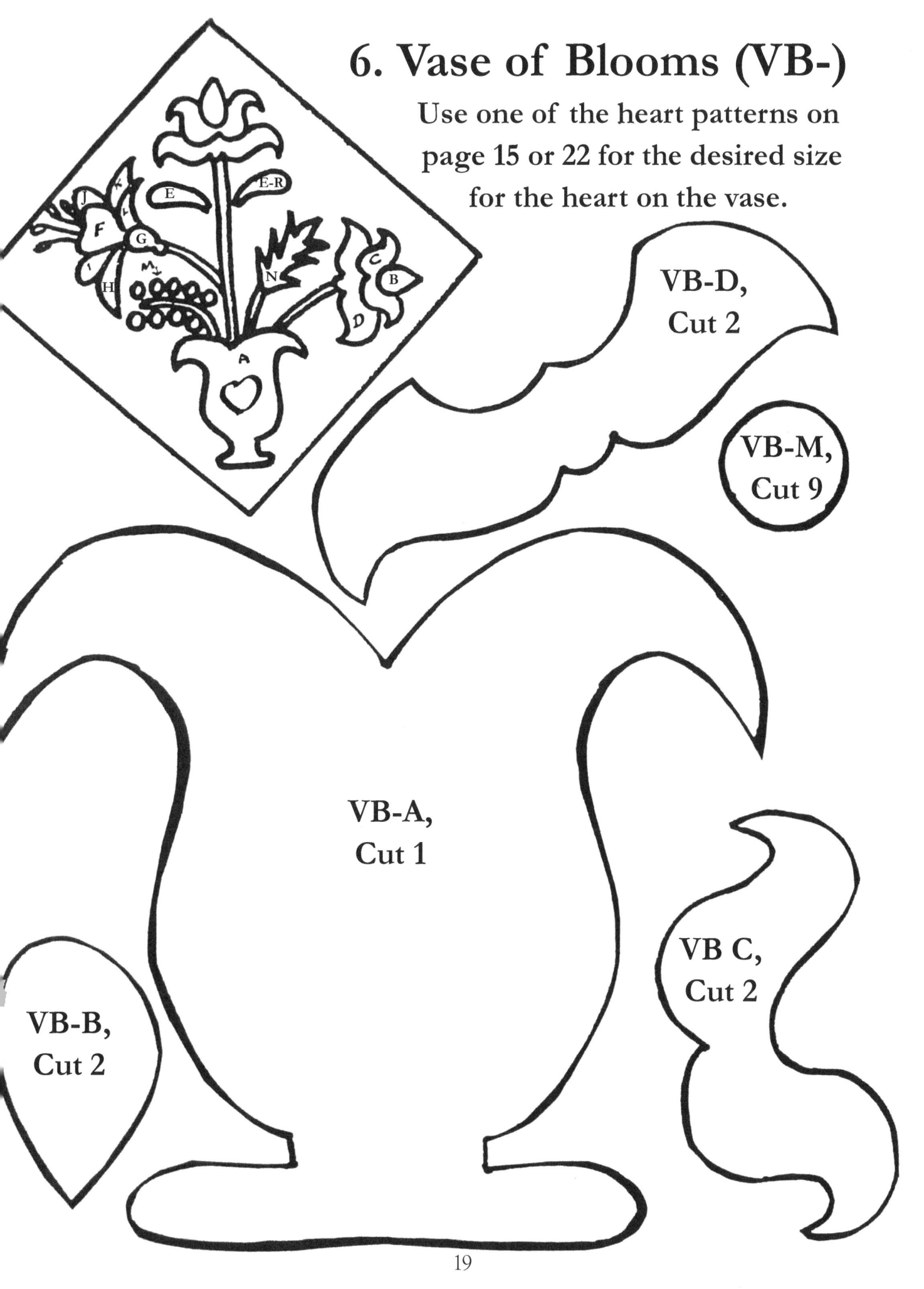

# 6. Vase of Blooms (VB-)

Use one of the heart patterns on page 15 or 22 for the desired size for the heart on the vase.

VB-D, Cut 2

VB-M, Cut 9

VB-A, Cut 1

VB-B, Cut 2

VB C, Cut 2

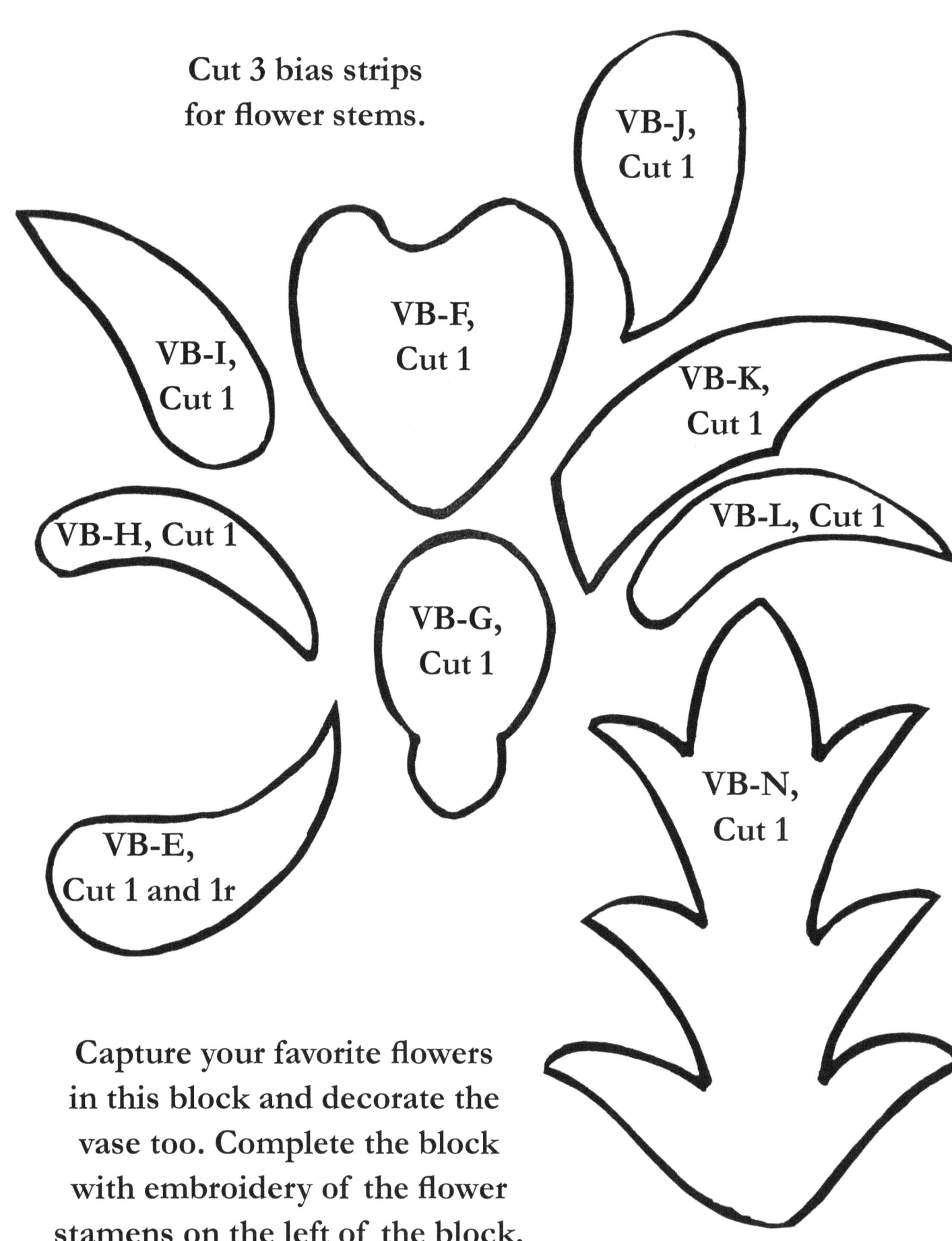

# Vase of Blooms

# 7. Love Bird (LB-)

Love birds sing the sweetest songs.

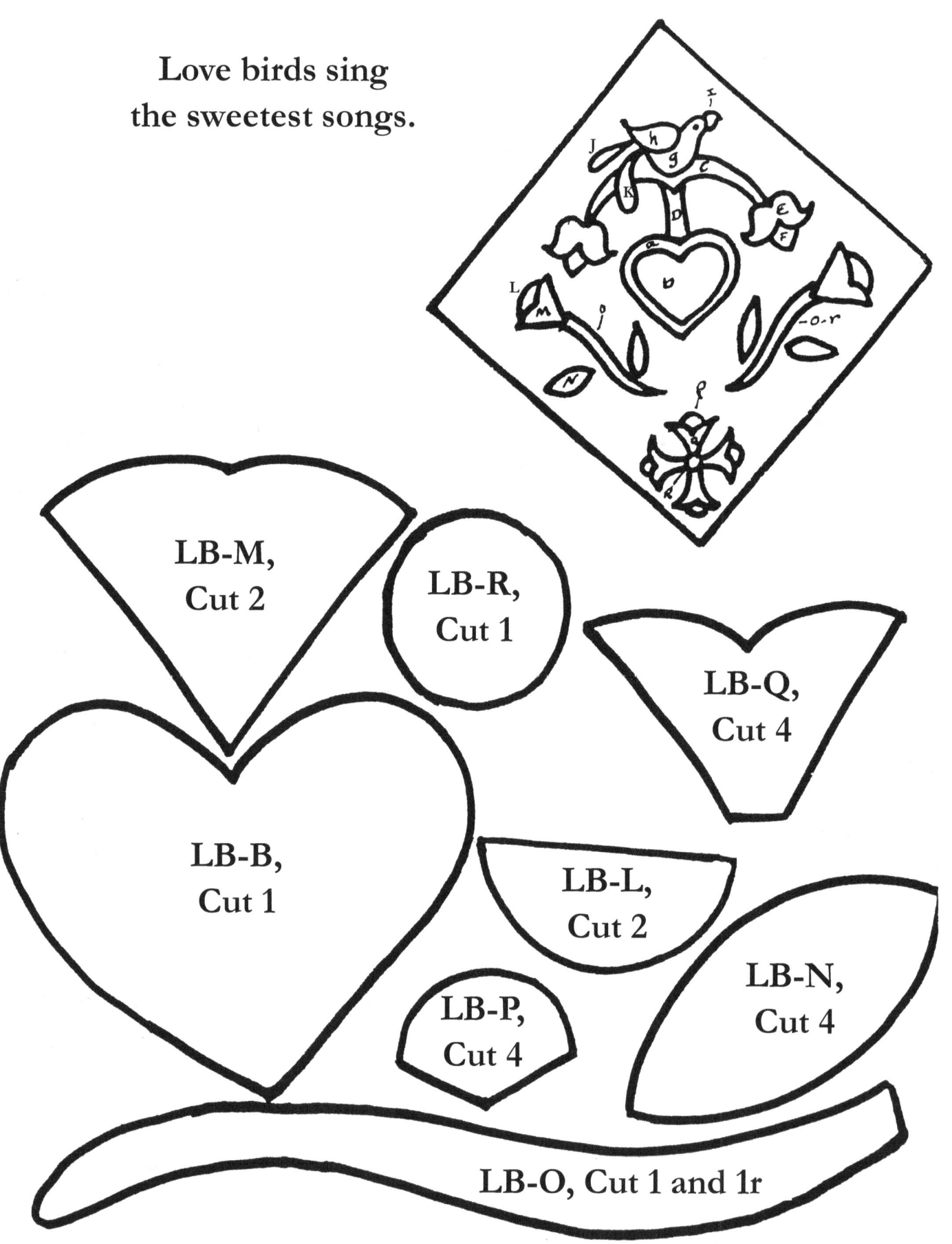

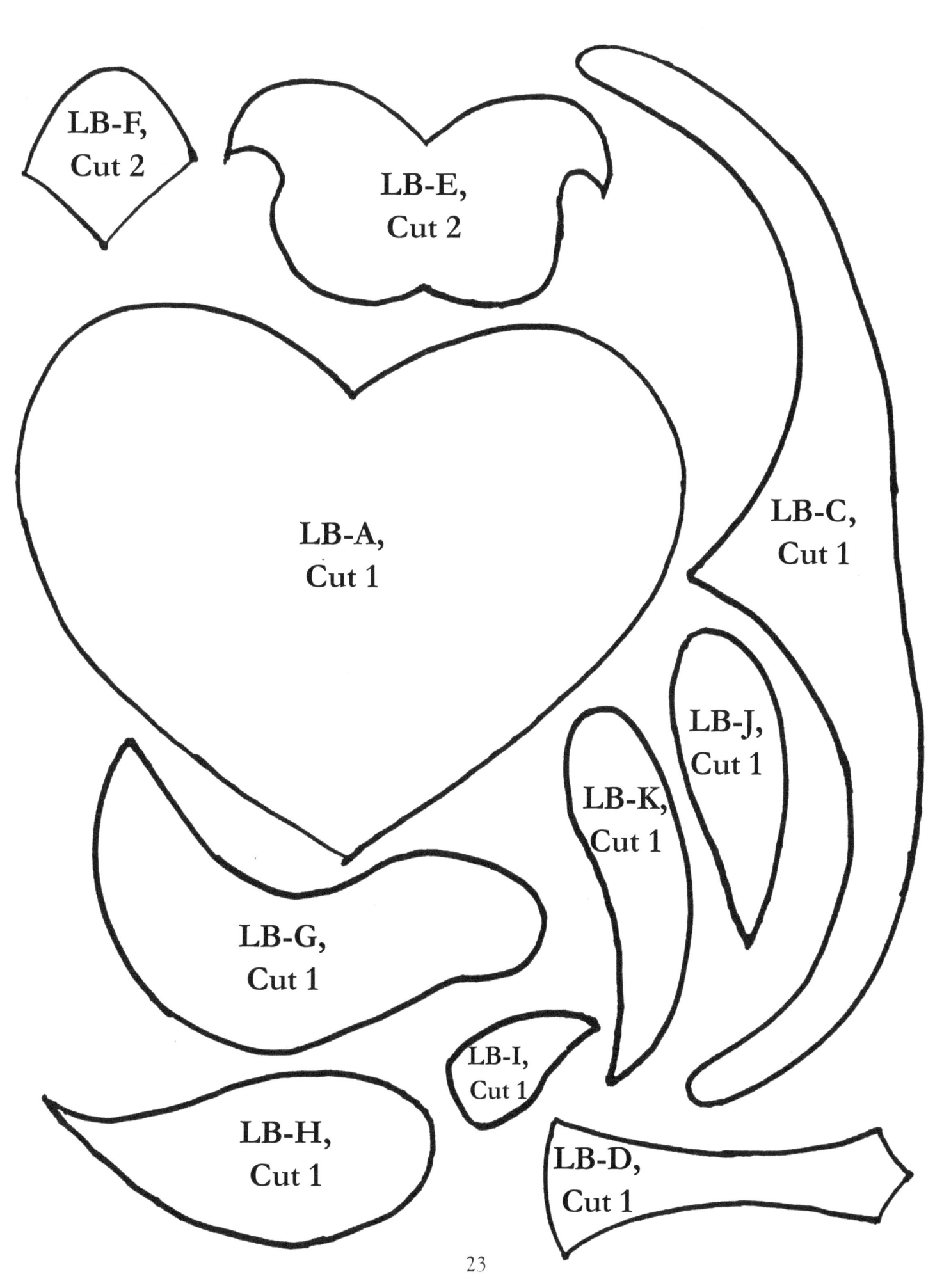

# Love Bird

# 8. Butterfly (BF-)

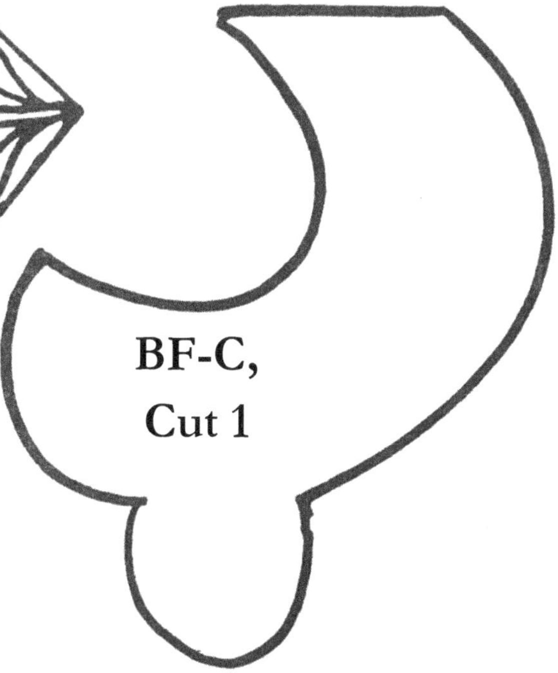

BF-C, Cut 1

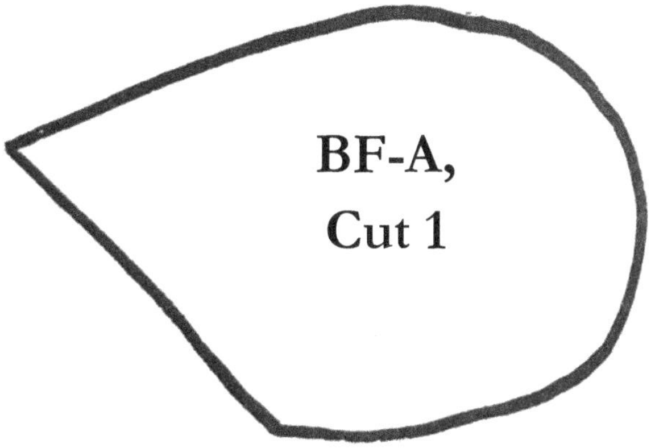

BF-A, Cut 1

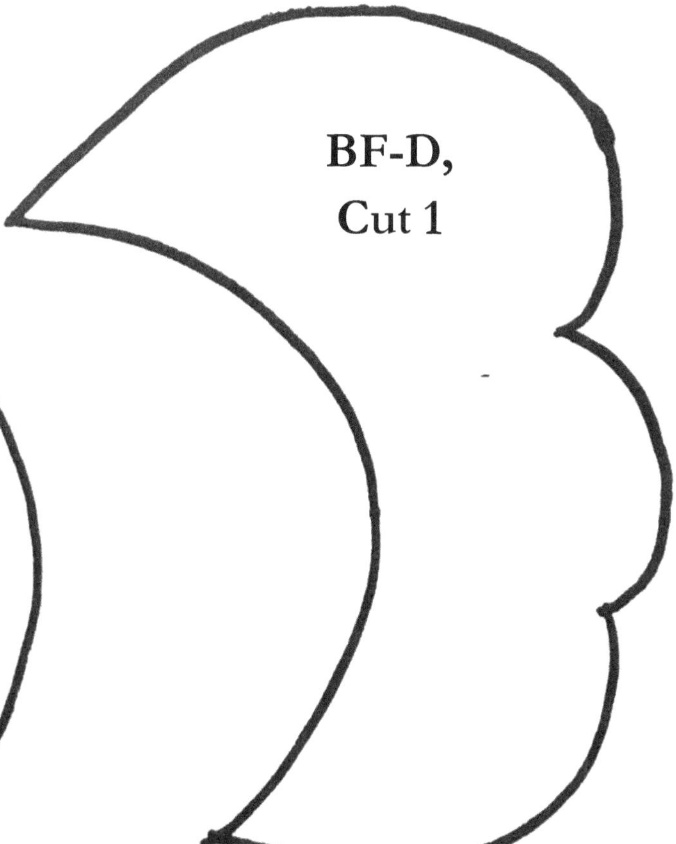

BF-D, Cut 1

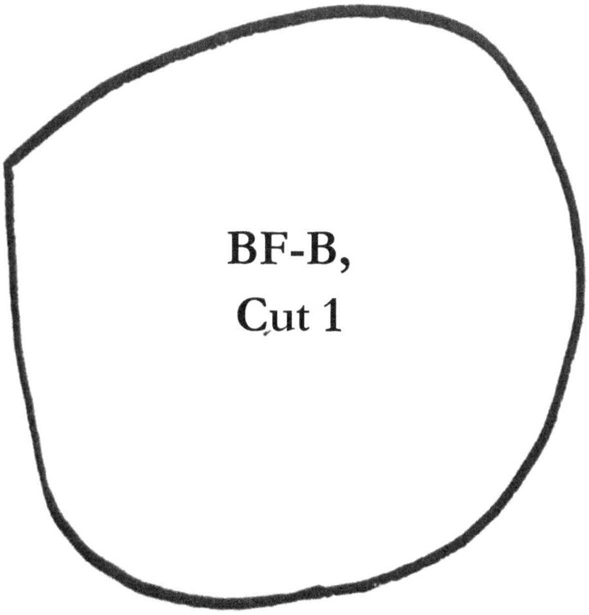

BF-B, Cut 1

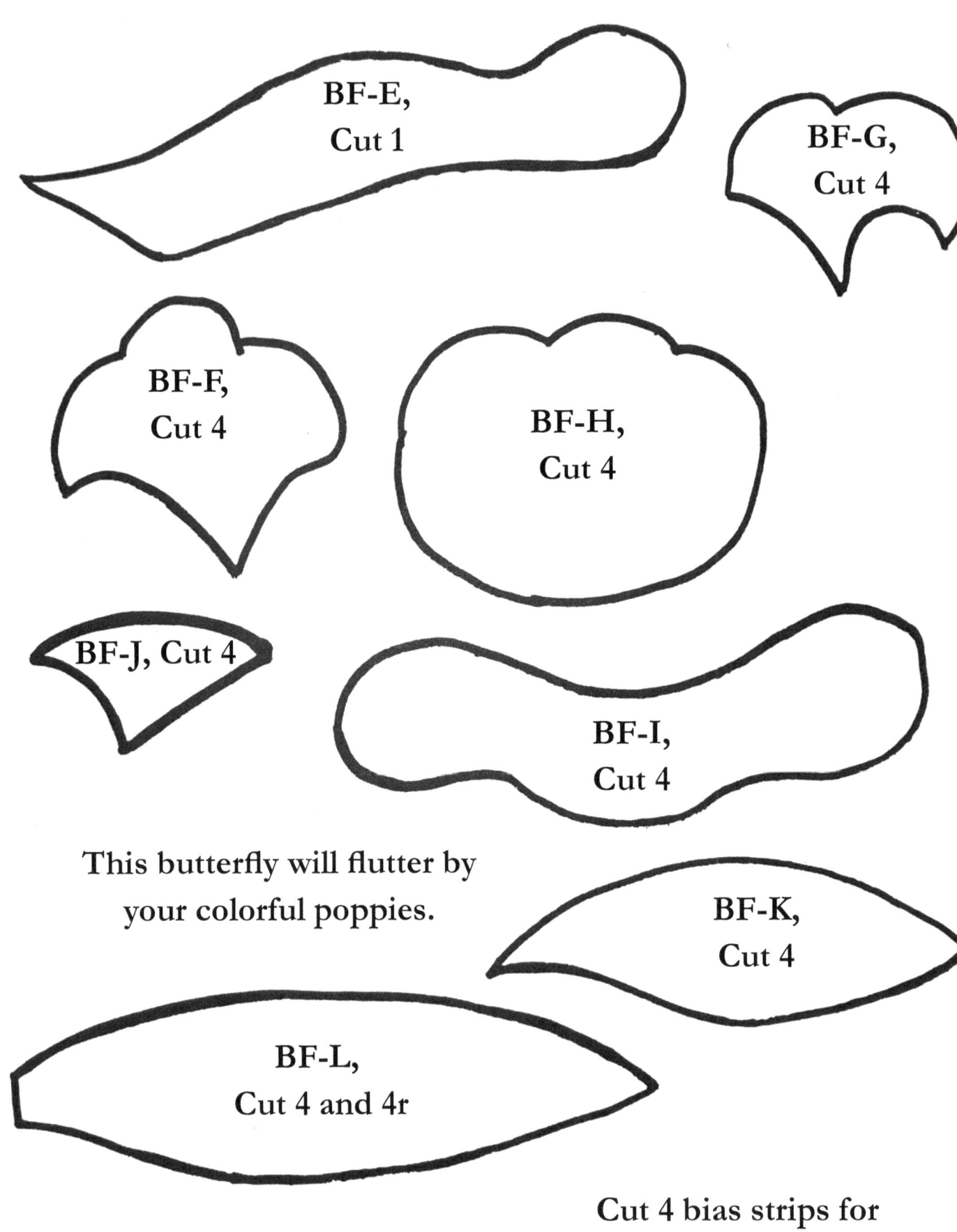

This butterfly will flutter by your colorful poppies.

Cut 4 bias strips for flower stems.

# Butterfly

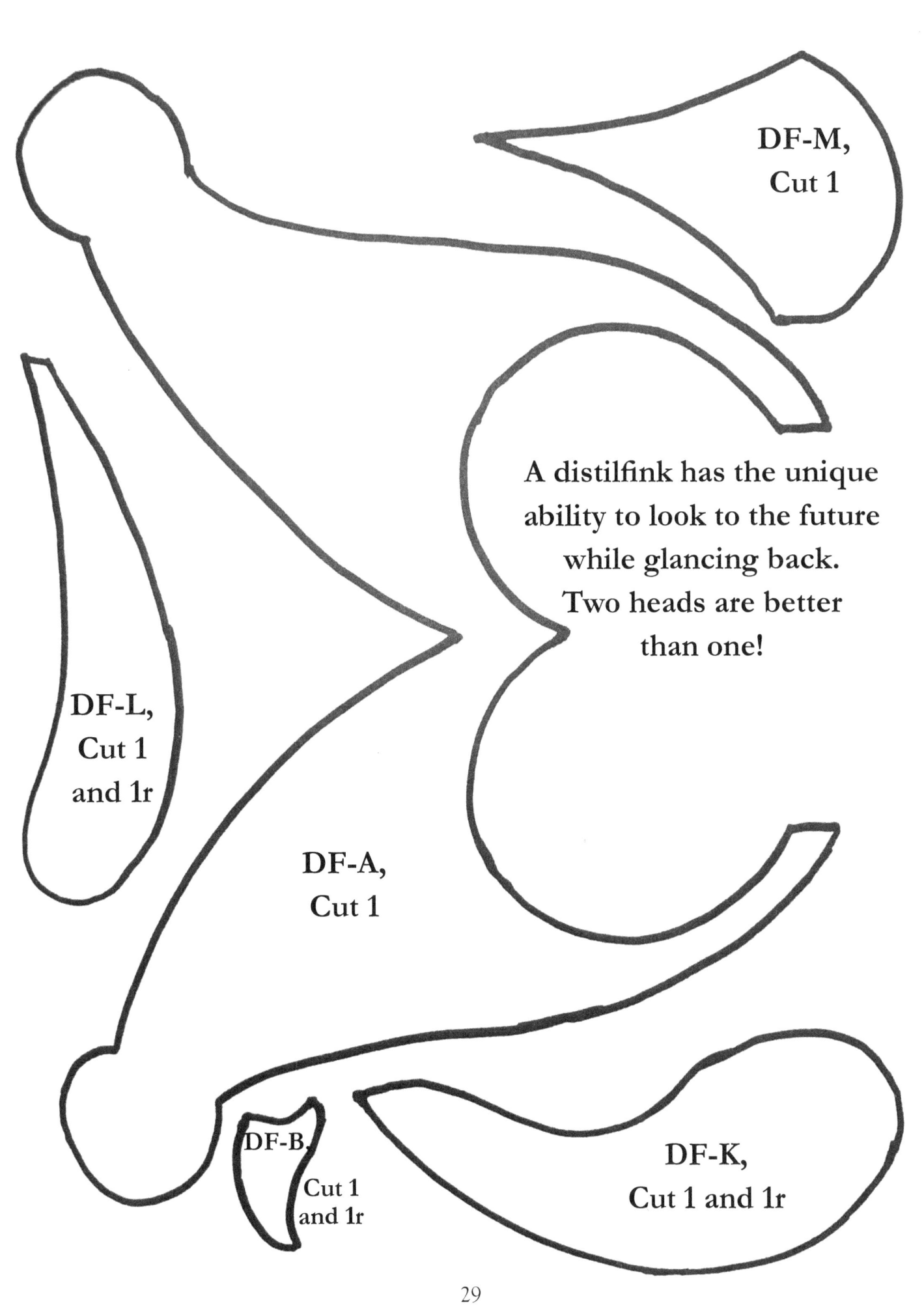

# Distilfink

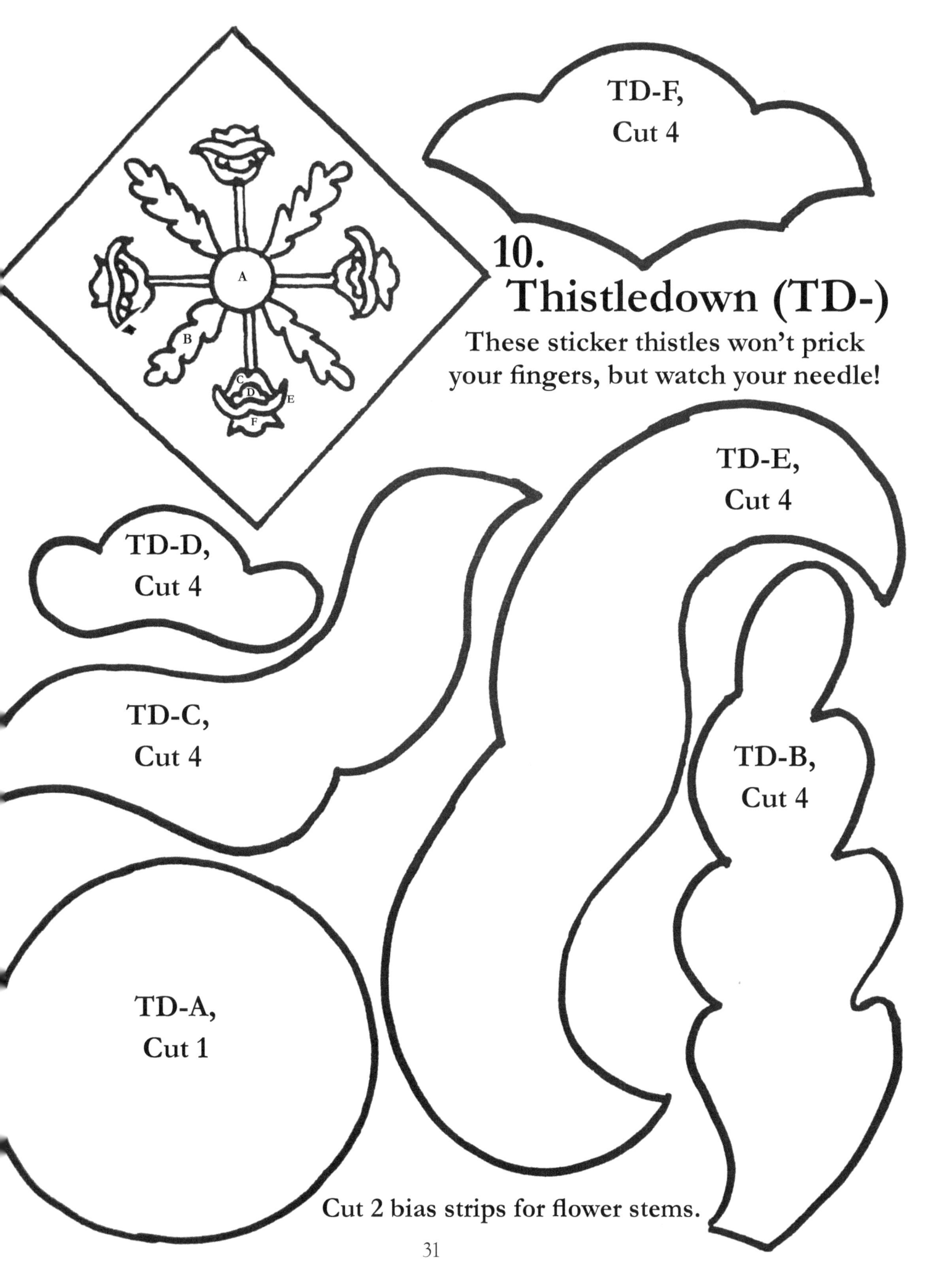

# 10. Thistledown (TD-)

These sticker thistles won't prick your fingers, but watch your needle!

TD-F, Cut 4

TD-E, Cut 4

TD-D, Cut 4

TD-C, Cut 4

TD-B, Cut 4

TD-A, Cut 1

Cut 2 bias strips for flower stems.

# Thistledown

# 11. Autumn Mums (AM-)

'Mum's the word' but these bright flowers are hard to ignore.

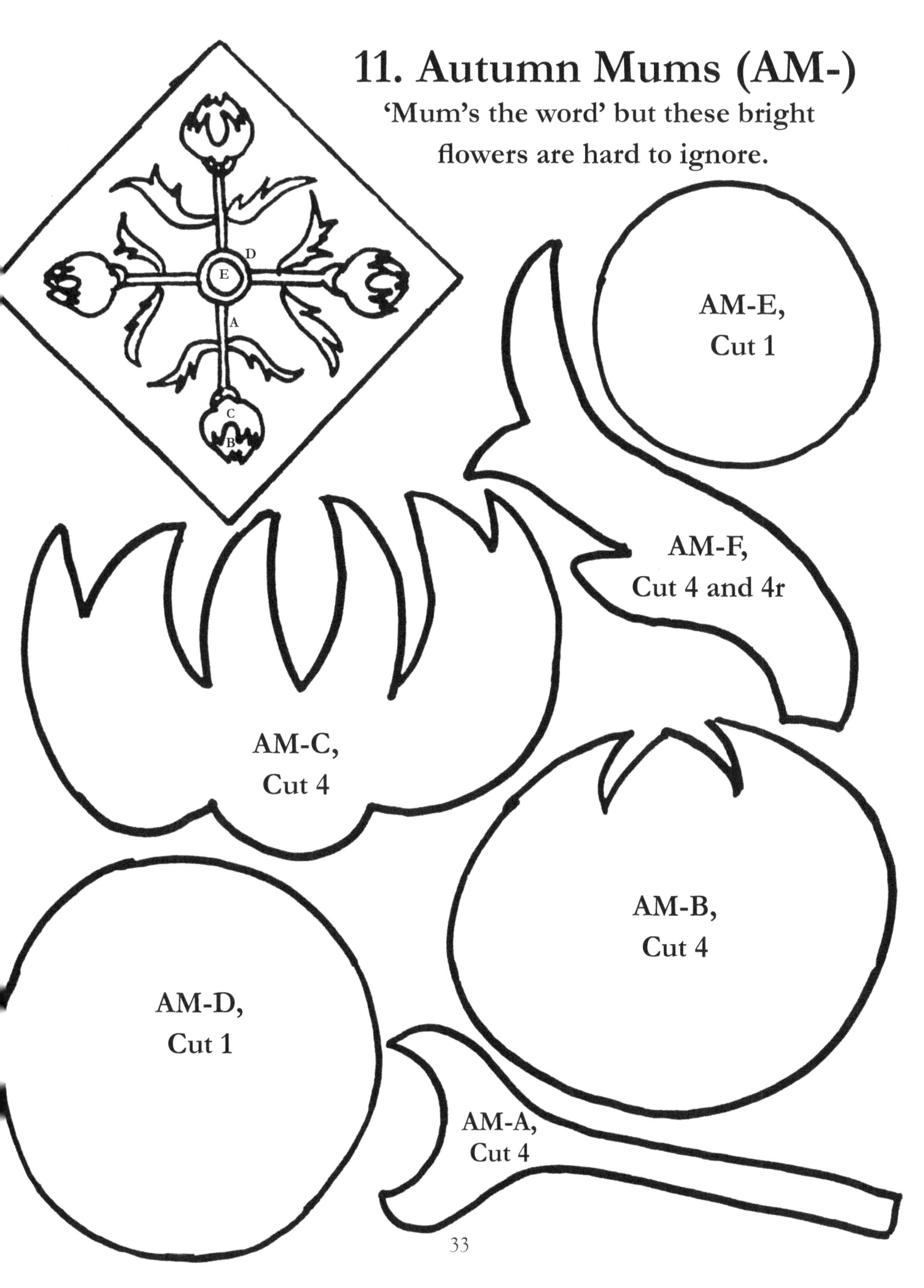

# Autumn Mums

# 12. Holiday Tulips (HT-)

Tulips are great any time of the year.

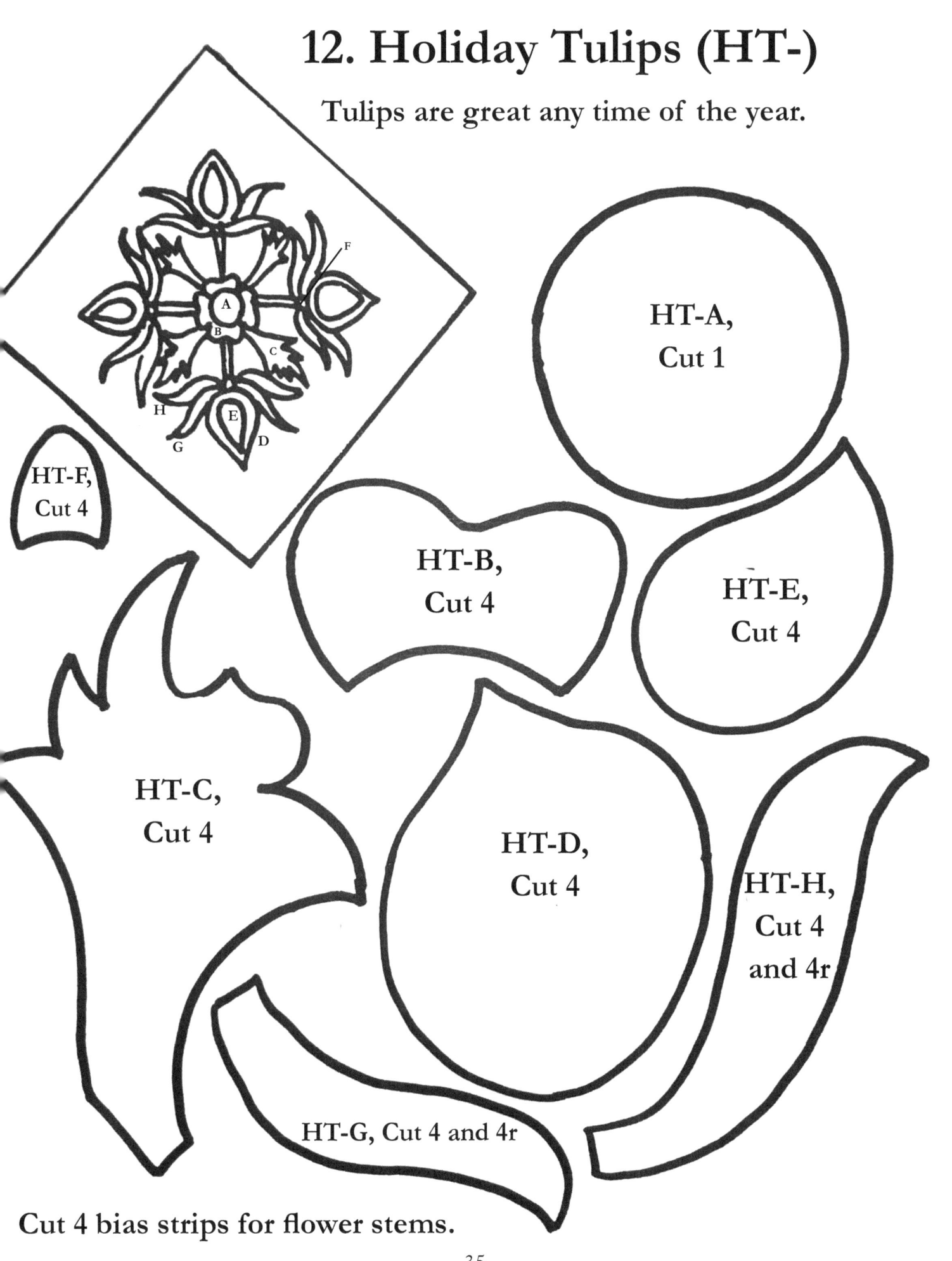

Cut 4 bias strips for flower stems.

# Holiday Tulips

# Border Templates

See cover photograph for placement suggestions.

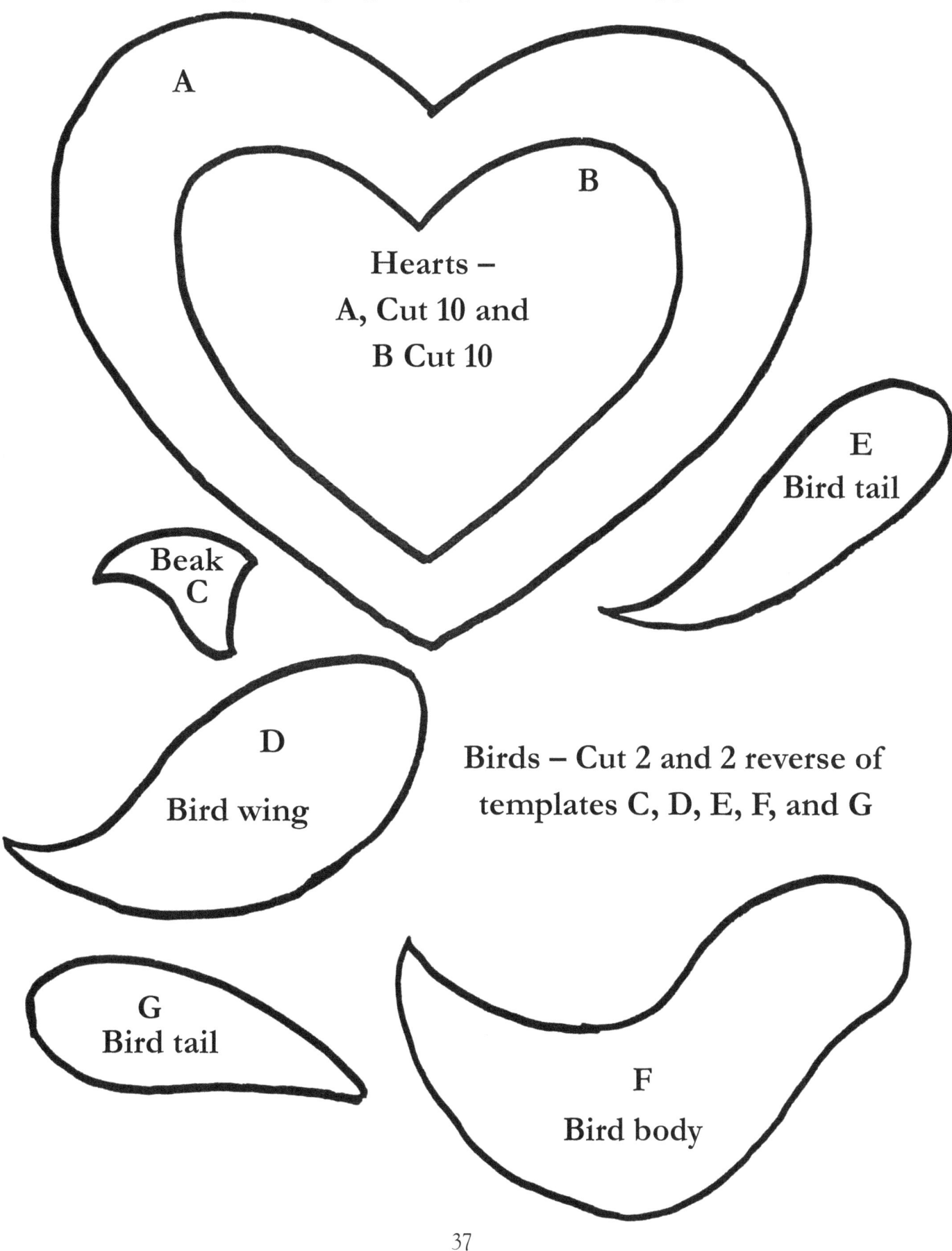

# Border Templates (cont.) Butterflies

Cut 2 of each butterfly parts H, I, J, K, and L for top and bottom quilt borders.

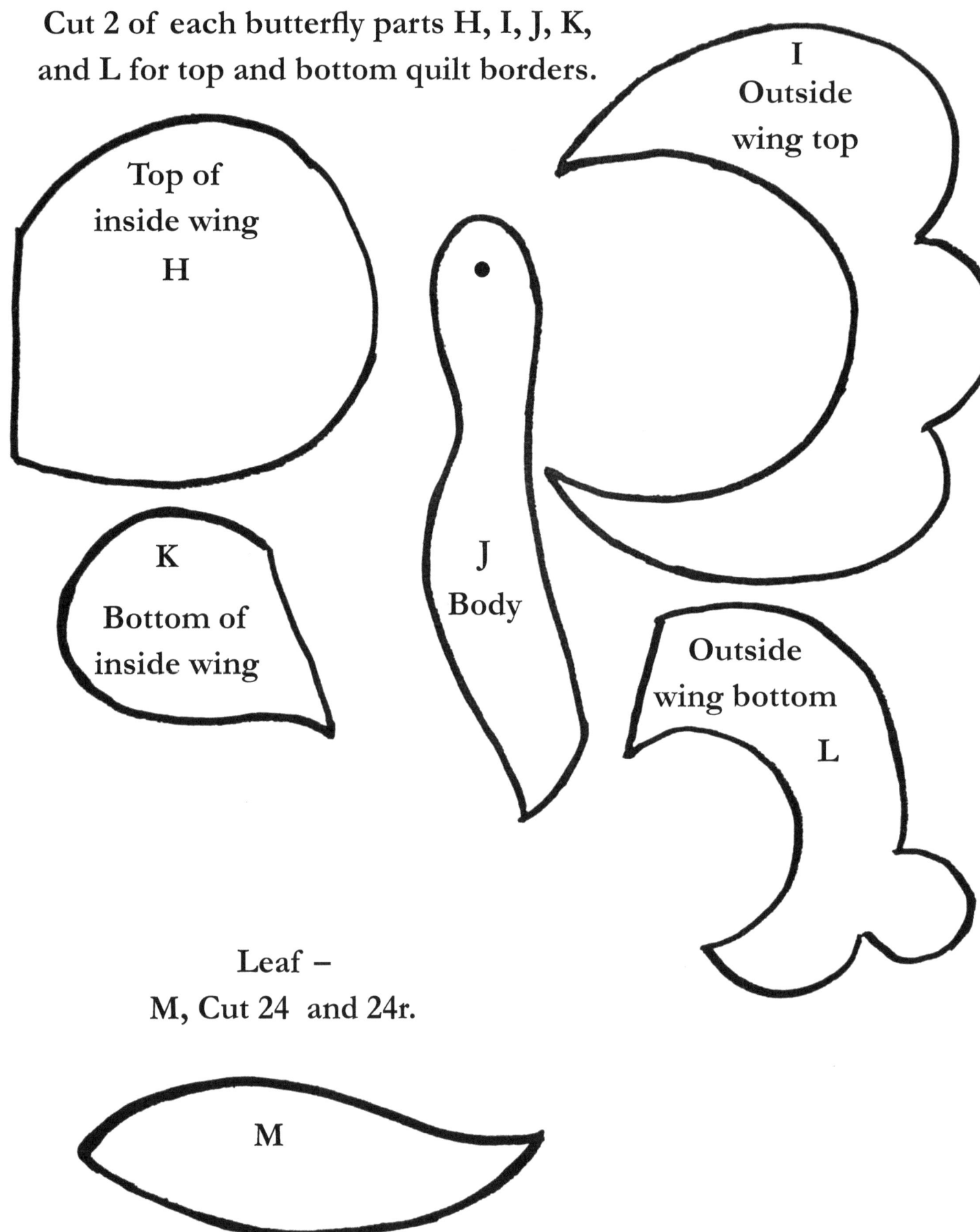

Top of inside wing H

I Outside wing top

K Bottom of inside wing

J Body

Outside wing bottom L

Leaf – M, Cut 24 and 24r.

M

# Border Flowers

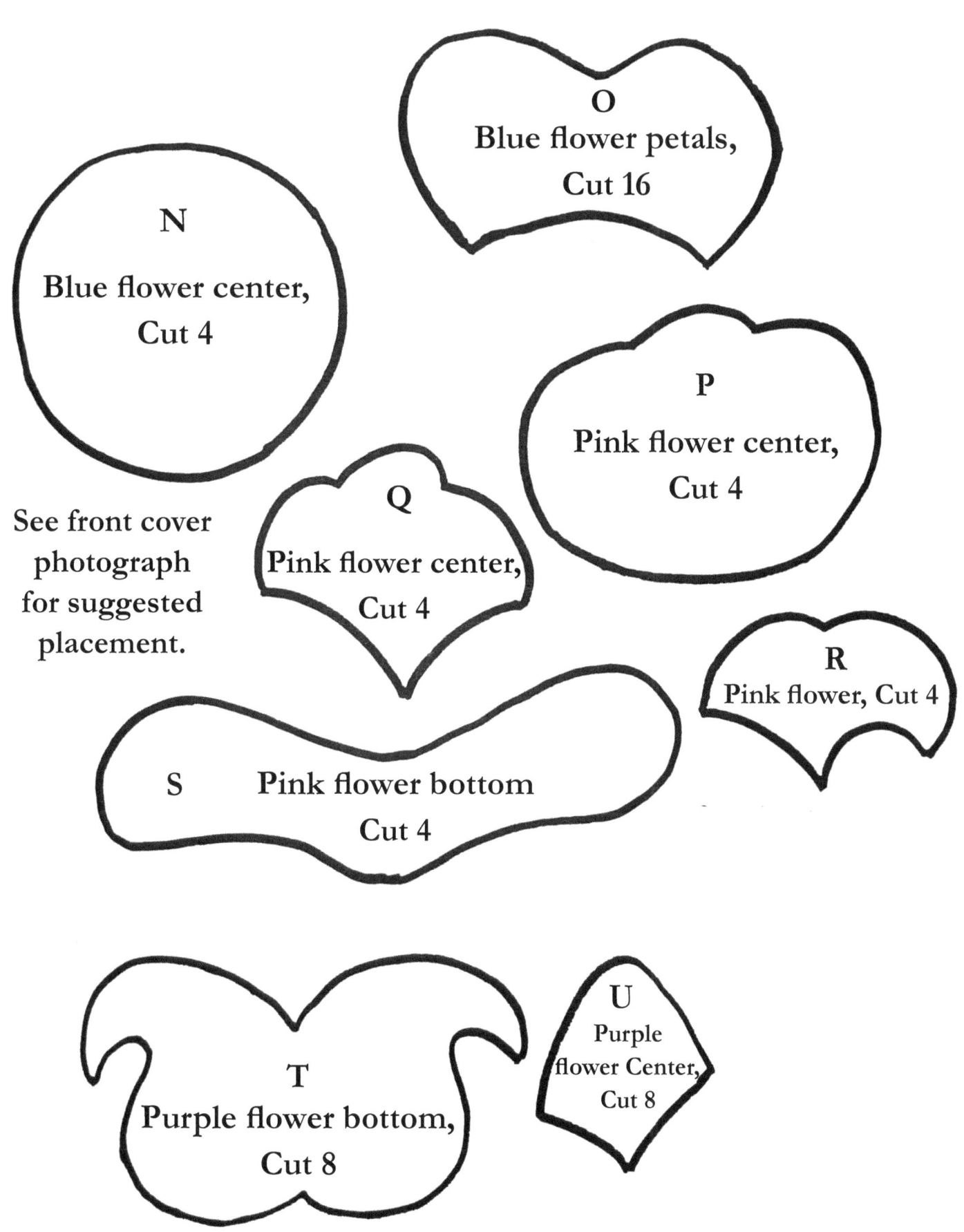

# Borders

# About Templates

Since this is a sampler quilt, you will accumulate quite a few templates. Plastic template material is recommended since it is transparent, lightweight and easy to trace through. Place the plastic over the pattern pieces in this book. Use a grease pencil or template pencil to trace the lines onto the plastic. Use a straight edge whenever necessary. For curves – keep your eye watching ahead of your pencil.

Don't cut the plastic with your sharp sewing scissors. The plastic will dull the cutting edge. Use paper scissors or an exacto knife to cut out the pieces. Don't mark another line for the seam allowance. These are finished sizes. The seam allowance will be added while cutting out the pieces as explained in the 'Marking and Cutting the Pattern' section below.

A small piece of adhesive or masking tape on the back of the plastic templates will keep them from slipping while marking the fabric. Mark the template for identification and note with an 'r' when pieces are to be reversed.

# Placement of Appliqué

Fold the muslin square into quarters and crease it, then unfold and crease it diagonally both directions. This will show a spider web of creases which will define how to place the pattern.

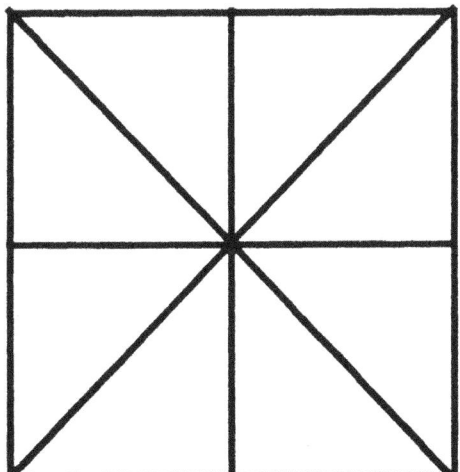

# Marking and Cutting the Pattern Pieces

Place the template pieces on the <u>right side</u> of the fabric. Trace around the template leaving enough space between the pieces to add a ¼ inch margin. <u>Don't</u> cut the fabric on the marked line. Instead, cut approximately ¼ inch on the outside of the marked line. To help with placement the pattern may be marked onto the background fabric using a water soluble marker. If desired, you may use a square of newsprint to mark the pattern in dark ink. Then place the background block over the newsprint marked pattern. Then trace the pattern onto a background block.

The first block is the Floral Hex. It is the block which will set the tone of your quilt colors. Most quilters have made this similar to the quilt's color wheel displaying the maker's color choices.

# Basting

The secret to good crisp appliqué is in basting. Clip along curves to aid the turning under process.

Thread the needle with 18 inches of quilting thread. To make the quilter's knot, hold the needle with the point up in the left (or non-dominant) hand. With the right hand (or dominant) hand hold the end of the thread and place it next to the needle with the eye down. Hold the thread on the needle between the left (non-dominant hand) thumb and finger. Pull up on the needle and pull the knot down to the end of the thread. If there is a tail of thread below the knot, clip it off. Otherwise, the knot will pull through fabric but the tail will show.

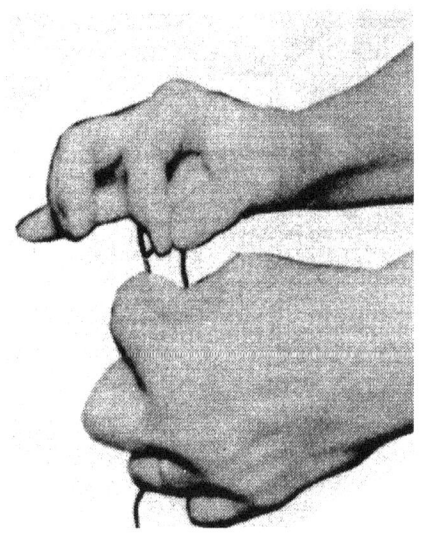 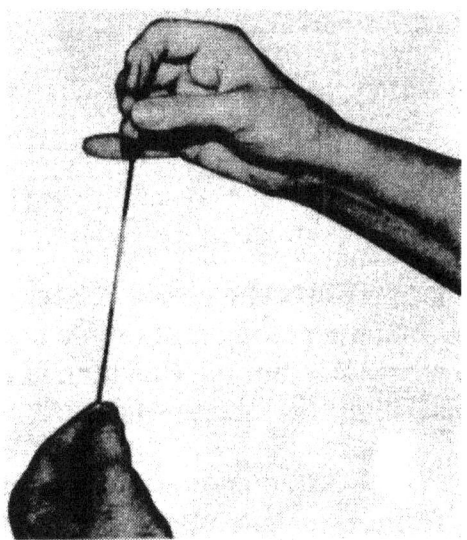

First, single-thread a contrasting colored thread through your needle. Knot it on the right side of the fabric. Make a running stitch on top of the marked seam line. Turn under the edges along the stitches and baste down the hem on the right side of the fabric. Again place your knot on the right side. Pull out the first bastings. Place the piece on the background muslin. Pin it in place on the marked muslin background then baste it down.

# Appliqué Stitching

Use the appliqué 'blind' stitch to fasten the pieces onto the background muslin square. This is a stitch which should not be visible. Choose a thread the same color, or as close as possible, to the piece being appliquéd onto the background block. Thread the needle and knot it with the quilter's knot as described above in the basting section. Come up from the bottom of the block to the very edge of the piece. Pull the thread through so the knot is snug on the back. Catch a small amount of the background fabric on the appliqué piece. Aim the needle so it is at a slight angle from the background to the appliqué piece. The point of the needle should be no more than a minute thread away from where the end of the thread comes through the piece. Go forward about 1/16 of an inch and come up along the edge. Pull the thread snug. Repeat the process until the piece is stitched down. The stitches on the back should show one slanted minute stitch and one straight small stitch. The front shouldn't show any noticeable stitches. Continue all around the piece. Knot the thread on the back by making a loop and pulling the thread through.

Pull out any bastings when finished. The appliquéd piece will look like it was always meant to be placed there. Turn the block to the wrong side. Use appliqué scissors to cut out the background block above and below the seam allowance. The 'bill' on the appliqué scissors will prevent you from cutting the front of your block. Carefully cut so no more than ¼ inch remains on the inside of the seams. Be careful to not cut the appliquéd pieces. This will make the block so that it isn't as thick when quilting it.

# Setting

All the blocks should be marked so that the pattern is 'on point.' This means when set together, all the filler blocks are also 'on point.' Before setting in the filler blocks, use a water-soluble pen and mark them with a quilting pattern. Mom suggested using the feather pattern on page 47.

Follow the setting procedure as illustrated on the previous page. Start at the upper left corner with a small triangle. Sew on an appliquéd block, then a filler block, another appliquéd, another filler, an appliquéd then an 18 ¼ inch triangle.

Make similar strips as illustrated. Then sew the strips together.

Measure the quilt top and cut the eight inch borders to fit the top, bottom and sides. Appliqué border patterns. Sew them on and miter the corners.

# Preparing to Quilt

After the top is completely appliquéd, the filler blocks are marked and everything is set together including the appliquéd borders, you are ready to prepare to quilt. The first step is to press the quilt top.

Choose a backing piece, probably white muslin. Measure at least one inch larger than your top all the way around. If you plan on using self-binding, then leave two inches all around.

Purchase the batting the size of your quilt. Different lofts, or thicknesses, of batting are manufactured. Polyester traditional batting is recommended because it is easier to sew through than high loft and puffier than low loft. Batting is generally packaged according to finished quilt size. Thus a queen size batting is appropriate for this project. Batting can also be purchased by the yard. If it is prepackaged, then remove it from the package to let it 'breathe' overnight. This allows it to puff naturally and takes some of the creases out.

Place the backing piece on the floor with the right side down. Lay the batting over the top of it. Start in the middle and pat out any wrinkles. Don't pull on the batting, because you will stretch it too thin. Patting will generally move it into position. Place the quilt top on the batting with the right side up. Start at one end and begin rolling the three layers as illustrated on the next page.

The rolling goes smoother with two people. As you roll watch the back for any wrinkles and pull them to the outside of the roll by tugging on the side of the backing. When the layers are rolled up pick up the roll and place it on a table. Unroll to the center. Pin about six inches apart starting in the center and progressing to the outside. Baste it in the same manner. Remove the pins. Roll up this side and unroll the other side. Pin and baste the second side in the same manner.

You are now ready to quilt. Start in the center. Make a quilter's knot. Pull the thread snug and work the knot through until it rests between the layers. Work in a widening circle to the outside. Use small even stitches outside each appliqué piece or following a marked pattern. Remember to use the quilter's knot to finish. Make a loop over your thumb, twist the loop as you pull it off your thumb and pull the threaded needle through the loop. Pull the knot down to the surface of the quilt top. Run the needle through the top layer about a ½ inch away and pop the knot into the layer to hide it. Pull the needle and thread up snug and clip the thread. The tail will disappear into the layer. Appliqué pieces should be quilted close to where they were sewn to the backing piece. This will allow them to puff up and will hide the 'blind' stitches even more.

If you smooth with your fingers as you go and work from the center to the outside, it is not necessary to use a hoop or quilt frame. This is called lap quilting.

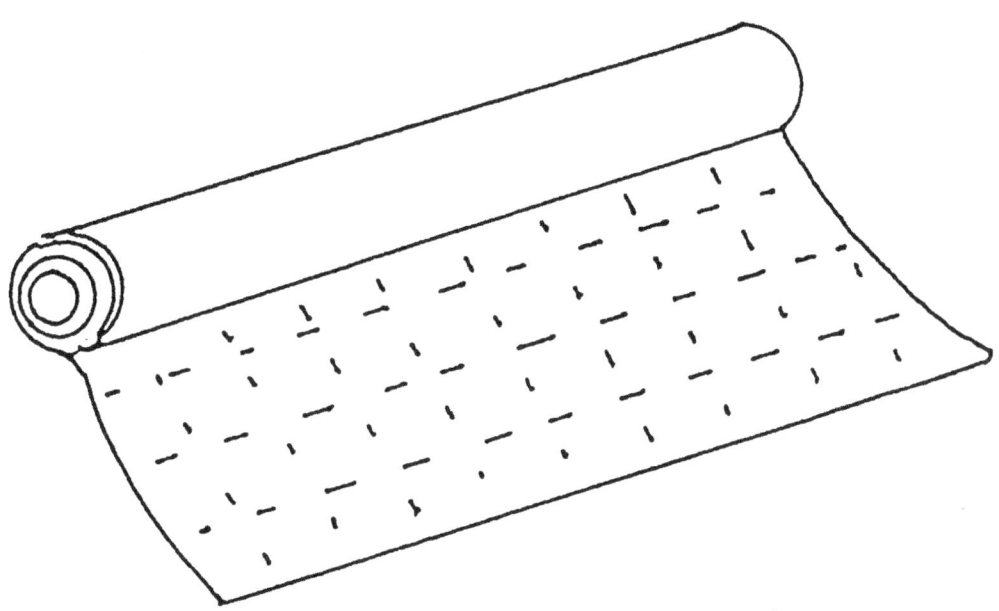

# Feather Pattern

To be used for filler blocks

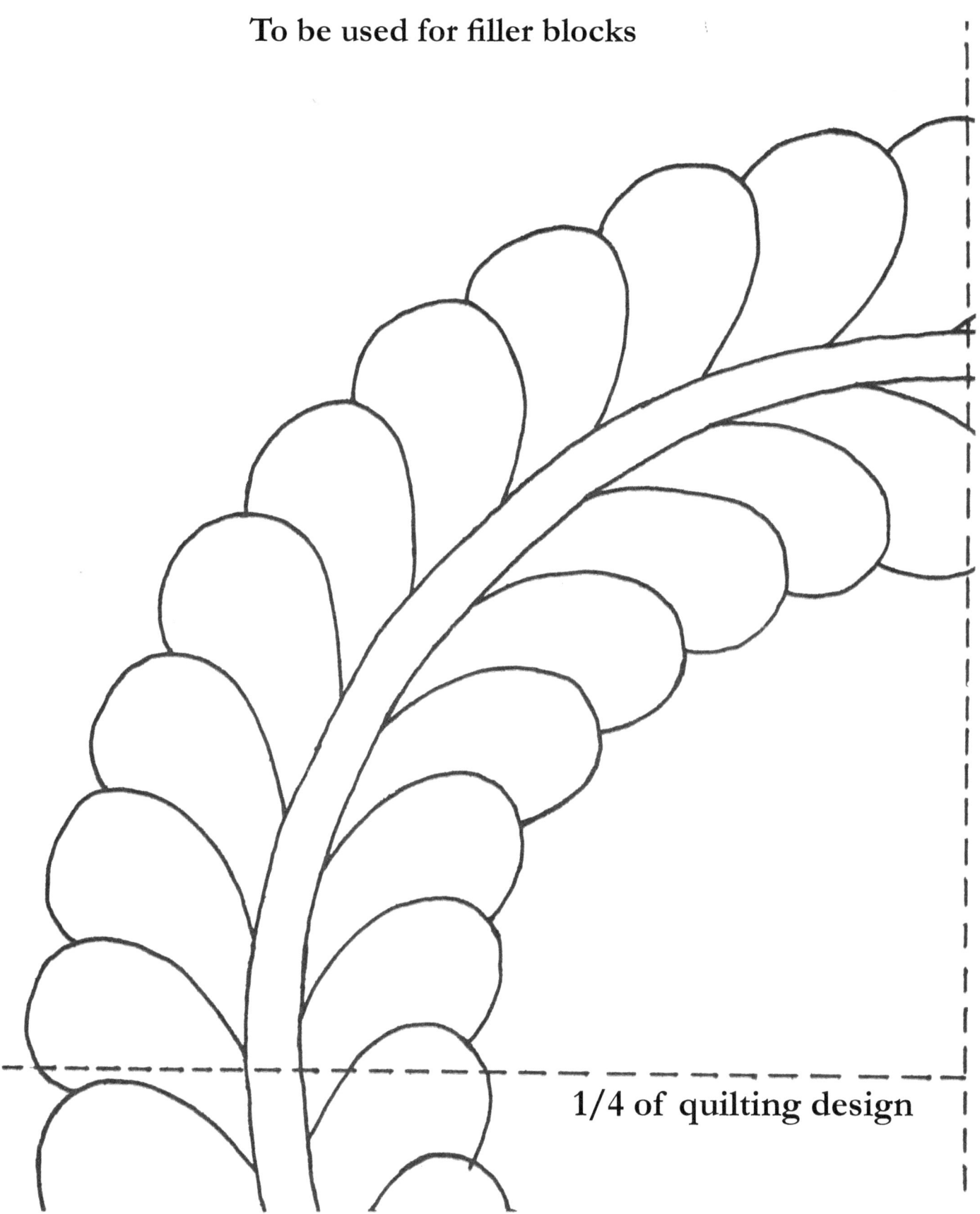

1/4 of quilting design

# Feather Wreath

# Finishing

The easiest way to finish is to use the self-binding method. It is important to plan ahead because two inches of backing fabric should be left all around. Trim the batting within an inch of the edges of the quilt. Turn the backing piece's raw edge under and blind stitch the backing to the front. Miter the corners because this makes them neat. It is important to keep some batting inside the binding in order to cut down on the amount of wear and tear on the quilt sides. The binding will probably wear out first, so this will help lengthen the life of the quilt. Also if you quilt along the inside edge of the binding, this will help prevent premature aging.

Another effective finishing method is to cut the bias binding 2 ½ inches wide. This particularly works if you don't want the backing to show on the front or if you prefer to use a framing type of binding. In order to cut continuous bias binding start with a square of fabric. One square yard will make 13 yards of bias. Cut the square diagonally in two. Sew it together as illustrated. Mark 2 ½ inch lines. Put the right sides together and offset the marks by one. Sew another seam to form a tube. Start cutting on the offset side and continue around until all the bias is cut.

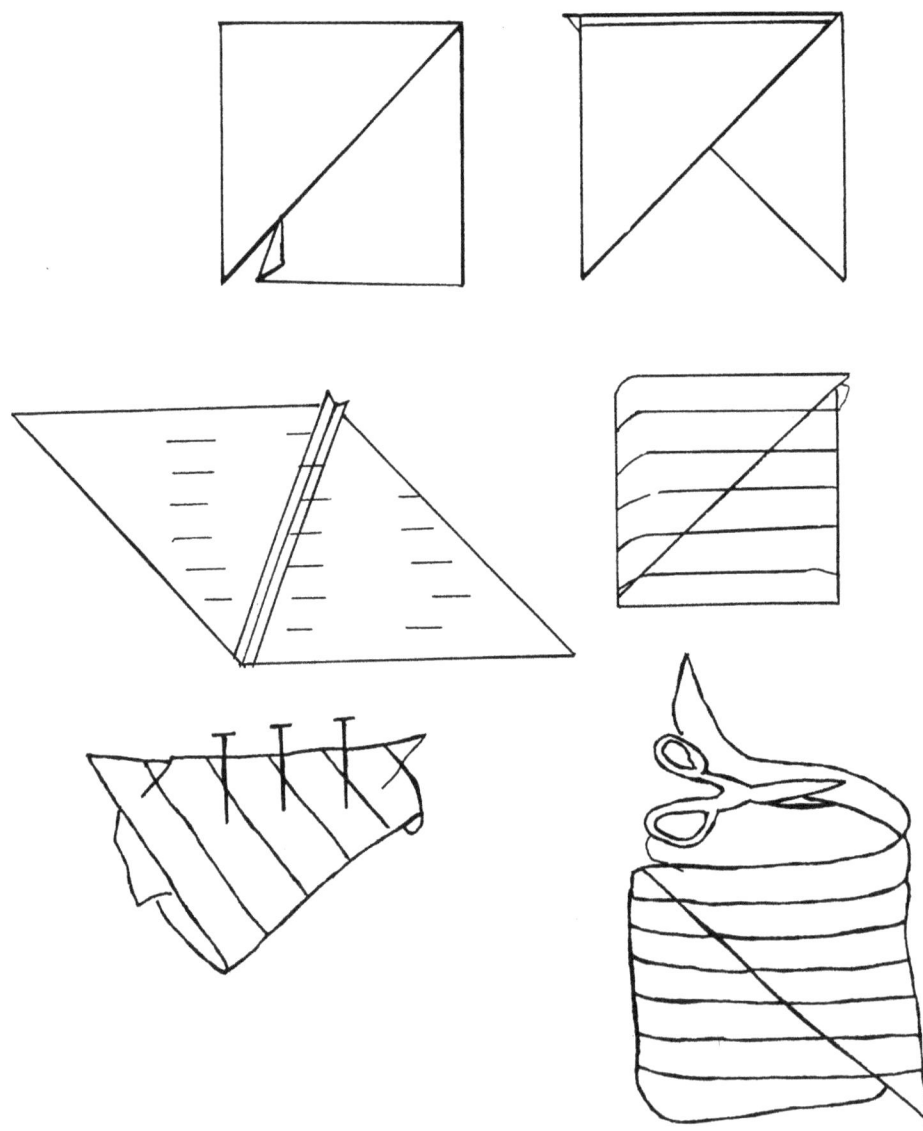

Fold the bias double and iron it. Trim the top and backing but leave about an inch of batting all around the quilt. Pin the raw edges to the raw edge of the quilt. Turn under and overlap the edges where the ends meet. Sew down either by hand or by sewing machine. Turn the folded edge to the back of the quilt. Pin it down. Miter the corners. Sew the bias tape down with a blind stitch.

After the quilt has been appliquéd and quilted, it needs to be washed to take out any water soluble ink. Don't use detergent when you are removing the ink, because it may cause a chemical reaction. Embroider your signature and date your masterpiece. You are now finished!

## Congratulations!

# Acknowledgments

I appreciate the help and encouragement I received in order to revive this book. I feel this honors my mother and her beloved craft.

Thank you to my husband Rob Klix who allows me the time I need to write. My son Scott Anderson lived with the quilt bug, which took over our family for a time. I'm glad he photographed more interior blocks and supported my decision to reprint this book. My daughter-in-law Kimberly McCarron Anderson provides me with help on my website as well as consultation for graphic design information.

Victoria Fletcher scanned the pattern pictures. I was very exacting about them needing to be the absolute right sizes. Thank you for your patience.

I am grateful to Jan Carol Publishing. Thank you Janie C. Jessee for embracing my vision to republish our quilt books. I'm sure Mother would be as proud as I am for this revision. Tara Sizemore has been an absolute wizard with pattern placement and template sizing.

Lastly thank you to all of the quilters I met over the years working with Mom. Their enthusiasm was palatable and their quilting efforts amazing. Thank you for continuing this ancient craft. I know many of Mom's students are still actively involved in the Black Hills Quilters' Guild.

# About the Author

Rose Klix, born and reared in Rapid City, South Dakota, loves the Black Hills, but also enjoys her current Appalachian foothills home in Tennessee. "The views inspire and renew me."

One day Rose observed her mother recommending sections in quilt books to her students. She asked, "Why don't you write your own book? Her mother answered, "You're the writer, you write the book for us."

"Mom spent extra time showing me each step of her process as I recorded her techniques in our first book *Adventures in Quilting* for beginner students." *More Adventures in Quilting* provided an intermediate level sampler project. *Folk Art Sampler Quilt* challenges appliqué quilters for an advanced project.

Rose welcomes visitors to her website www.RoseKlix.com to learn more about her, read book reviews, and link to her blog. The Contact page connects to her social media.

**Rose's current publications include:**

**Poetry:** *God, My Greatest Love* religiously and spiritually inspired moments; *Eat, Diet, Repeat* shares funny and poignant times of temptation to enjoy tasty choices. *Pastiche of Poetry Vol. I and II*, Rose's 50-year two-volume collection includes reflections of imagination and recollections of life experiences.

**Fiction:** *My Short and Long-Stemmed Stories* collects Rose's short fiction about ordinary people whether bowler or biker, widower, teenager, or newlywed, challenged through a variety of scenes and settings such as a retirement center, a tattoo parlor, or gambling online.

**New Age:** In *Past Lives Before Now* Rose shares twenty-three life journeys based on her soul memories explored through regressions. She discovers that all four elements of love provided the fullest lives in her past experiences.

"I'll keep writing until I have nothing more to say."

Watch for Rose's next publications.

www.ingramcontent.com/pod-product-compliance
Lightning Source LLC
Chambersburg PA
CBHW061815290426
44110CB00026B/2879